Deep Sea

10 Things You
Should Know

Jon Copley is Professor of Ocean Exploration and Science Communication at the University of Southampton, where his research as a marine biologist explores life in deep-sea environments around the world. He went on the first minisub dive to the world's deepest undersea hot springs, more than three miles deep on the ocean floor, and he has led expeditions discovering new species of deep-sea animals. Jon has worked with documentary makers to bring the exploration of the deep ocean to global audiences in TV series for the BBC and National Geographic, and often shares the reality of our deep ocean planet in popular science articles and talks at science festivals.

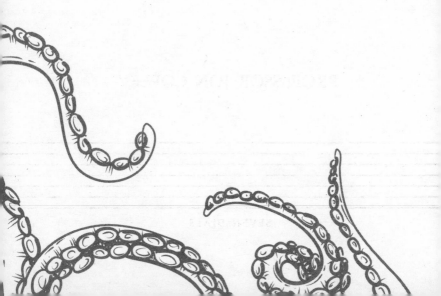

Deep Sea

10 Things You
Should Know

*A deep dive into one of the most
mysterious environments on our planet*

PROFESSOR JON COPLEY

SEVEN DIALS

First published in Great Britain in 2023 by Seven Dials
an imprint of The Orion Publishing Group Ltd
Carmelite House, 50 Victoria Embankment
London EC4Y 0DZ

An Hachette UK Company

1 3 5 7 9 10 8 6 4 2

A CIP catalogue record for this book is
available from the British Library.

ISBN (Hardback) 978 1 3996 1533 4
ISBN (eBook) 978 1 3996 1534 1
ISBN (Audiobook) 978 1 3996 1535 8

Typeset by Born Group
Printed in Great Britain by Clays Ltd, Elcograf S.p.A.

www.orionbooks.co.uk

Dedication

To Mum and Dad, always still with me even in the
darkest depths.

And to you, the reader, for taking the plunge into
the deep sea by picking up this book.

Contents

Prelude

A Kind of Harmony

Contents

Preface

The deep sea isn't what you think it is.

Even after a quarter-century of exploring it as a marine biologist, that statement still holds true for me. And that's what I love about the deep sea: the discoveries that we continue to make there are always expanding our perspective of life and how our planet works.

I became a deep-sea biologist through a chance encounter with a book in a library, when a photo of some strange-looking animals caught my eye on the cover of a volume on a shelf. They were unlike anything I'd seen before: worm-like animals with feathery red plumes poking out of white tubes on dark basalt rocks somewhere under the sea. I fetched down the book and found it was a collection of research papers about species that thrive at hot springs on the ocean floor, which were quite a recent discovery at the time.

As I read about how those deep-sea animals over-turned rules of biology that I'd just learned at school, I was instantly hooked by the realisation that we could still discover such astounding things in the deep sea. And although this book doesn't have pictures like the one that caught my eye, I've included the formal scientific names of species so that anyone can find the latest and best footage of them that scientists have shared online.

The phenomena and species that we've recently discovered are helping to build an even better understanding of 60 per cent of our planet that is covered by the deep sea. They also provide a continual reminder of how nature is more rich and complex than we can imagine. And as a result of my own deep-sea journey, I now try to look at nature around me as if I were encountering it for the first time on a dive, to realise how our everyday world is as astonishing as what's down there.

I hope this book takes you into the deep, even just for a couple of hours while reading it, and that you don't come back quite the same from the journey either.

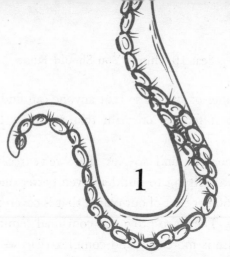

1

We Know Much More About the Deep Sea Than the Moon or Mars

Stroll out after dark on a clear night, and you can glance up at the sky to wonder about the stars and planets scattered above you. But you can't take a casual glance into the deep sea like that, even though it is much closer to us than the depths of space. Perhaps because it is out-of-sight, the deep sea has become a realm for creations of our imagination. Some of the names of its features evoke the dark underworld of our myths, from the 'abyssal plains' to the 'hadal environment' of ocean trenches. Recent Hollywood blockbusters, such as *The Meg* and *Underwater*, have also populated the deep sea with huge and ancient monsters, continuing themes explored more than a century earlier in Tennyson's *The Kraken* and HG Wells' *In the Abyss*.

Even in the world of non-fiction, the deep sea is typically portrayed as an unexplored frontier – admittedly a useful trope when it comes to chasing funding for deep-sea research – culminating in popular claims that we know more about the Moon or Mars than the ocean depths. But we actually know more about the deep sea than those other places in the Solar System. We have been exploring the deep sea for several centuries, collected far more samples and data from there than from other planets, and many more people and machines have visited the deep sea than space.

Deep Sea: 10 Things You Should Know

First of all, we should define what we mean by 'the deep sea'. The deep sea consists of all the parts of the ocean – the seafloor and the 'inner space' of mid-water – that lie more than 200 metres beneath the waves. That 200-metre upper boundary for the deep sea represents the maximum depth at which tiny drifting algae can grow, because sunlight becomes too dim for them to photosynthesise beyond that depth. It's also the average depth of the sea at the edge of the continental shelves that fringe the land, where the seabed starts to slope down into the ocean basins.

The oceans cover 71 per cent of the Earth, but, unlike the continents, they are all joined up with currents flowing between them, so we can think of our planet as having a single global ocean. And nearly all of that ocean is deep sea: its average depth is about 3,500 metres, and its deepest point is around 10,925 metres, at the Challenger Deep of the Mariana Trench in the Pacific. So our planet isn't just an ocean planet – the deep sea covers most of our world.

Our knowledge of the deep sea begins with measuring the depth of the seabed, and one of the earliest recorded measurements was reported by the Greek philosopher Posidonius of Rhodes just over 2,000 years ago, when he described lowering a weighted line to discover that the seabed was around 1,800 metres deep near Sardinia. Lowering weighted lines to measure depths continued for centuries, eventually leading to the first maps showing the undulations of the ocean floor in the second half of the nineteenth century. But lowering a weighted line to measure depth is a slow process, and each measurement is just one pinprick on the map. Fortunately the invention of echo sounding – bouncing pulses of sound off the seabed to measure its depth – in the early twentieth century has enabled much faster mapping of the ocean floor since then.

Unfortunately we can't map the terrain of the ocean floor directly using radar from satellites in the same way that we can map the surfaces of the Moon or Mars, because seawater blocks radar signals. However, satellites can measure tiny variations in the surface of the ocean, which represent the undulations of the seabed below, and that allows us to estimate the average depth of the global ocean. But satellite-derived maps of the ocean floor are much less detailed than the radar maps of the surfaces of the Moon and Mars. That's the only aspect in which we 'know more' about those other planets – we have more detailed maps of their terrain, because they are not covered by seawater.

To map the ocean floor to a similar level of detail as the Moon or Mars, we have to use sonar from ships instead of radar from satellites. Modern sonar systems map a narrow strip of seafloor beneath a ship as it crosses the ocean, and it takes a long time – and lots of planning – to map a region by joining up the narrow strips beneath ships' tracks. But just under a quarter of the global ocean floor has now been mapped in detail by sonar from ships – and that 90 million square kilometres is almost two-thirds the area of Mars and more than twice the area of the Moon's surface.

Making a map is just the start of exploration, and understanding what happens in the deep ocean, such as the geological processes that shape the seafloor, requires samples for scientists to analyse. Samples of the deep seafloor have been routinely collected since the nineteenth century, as part of mapping the deep using weighted lines, and they vastly outstrip the geological samples that have been collected or analysed from other planets. The total amount of rock that has been collected from the Moon to understand its geology is less than 500 kilograms. And apart from a few tiny pieces of Mars that have tumbled to Earth as a result of rare Martian meteorites, so far the only geological analysis of that world's rocks has been made by equipment aboard rovers on its surface.

The first species of an animal from the deep sea was described by naturalists in the 1760s – a stalked crinoid collected by Caribbean fishermen from more than 200 metres deep. Stalked crinoids are known as sea lilies, although they are animals related to starfish, and were previously only known as fossils, so their discovery in

Professor Jon Copley

the deep sea stimulated curiosity about what might live down there. The descriptions of other deep-sea species soon followed: the naturalist George Shaw described the tube-eye fish *Stylephorus chordatus* in 1791, for example, noting its huge upward-looking eyes that are common in animals where it lives between 300 and 800 metres deep. And in the early 1800s, Antoine de Risso described species fished up on long-lines from as much as 1,000 metres deep in the Mediterranean, including the dragonfish *Stomias boa*, which has rows of bioluminescent lights on its body typical of many mid-water deep-sea animals. So we have known about deep-sea animals for longer than we have known about dinosaurs, as the word 'dinosaur' wasn't coined until 1842. Meanwhile our knowledge of life on other worlds remains theoretical, and much of our understanding of the limits for life elsewhere in the cosmos has come from exploring life in the deep sea.

When it comes to sending machines and people into the ocean, the exploration of the deep sea is also far ahead of the Moon or Mars. To explore the deep ocean, we have three types of vehicles: Human-occupied Vehicles (HOVs), Remotely Operated Vehicles (ROVs), and Autonomous Underwater Vehicles (AUVs). As their name implies, Human-occupied Vehicles can carry people, and William Beebe and Otis Barton made the first HOV dive into the deep sea in 1930, reaching 435

9

metres deep in a vehicle called the bathysphere. In 1932 they broadcast live on the radio from the bathysphere at 671 metres deep, describing what they were seeing to audiences across the US and UK three decades before televised Moon landings. In 1934 they reached 923 metres deep, and their colleague Gloria Hollister also became the first female 'bathynaut' on a dive to 368 metres deep. After those pioneering bathysphere dives, other increasingly sophisticated HOVs visited greater depths, and Jacques Piccard and Don Walsh became the first people to reach the ocean's deepest point – more than 10 kilometres down in the Challenger Deep of the Mariana Trench – aboard the bathyscaphe *Trieste* in 1960.

Around 600 people have travelled into space since Yuri Gagarin's first orbit of the Earth aboard *Vostok-1* in 1961, but many more people have visited the deep sea than space. It's hard to keep count because there have been so many vehicles carrying people into the deep sea over the years, but it's certainly in the tens of thousands. And on 23 June 2020, the number of people who have dived to the very deepest place in the ocean overtook the number of people who have walked on the Moon.

Remotely Operated Vehicles (ROVs) don't carry people but are connected to a ship by a long tether cable, relaying live video and enabling operators to pilot them and collect samples with their mechanical arms. ROVs have been routinely used for deep-sea science since the 1990s, and Japan's *Kaiko* ROV made nineteen dives to the bottom of the Mariana Trench between 1995 and 1998. While there are currently two Mars rovers sending back data from the surface of the Red Planet, there are many more ROVs dangling from research ships at any one time, as part of expeditions exploring the deep sea around the world.

Autonomous Underwater Vehicles (AUVs) monitor the ocean depths, but aren't remotely controlled – instead they undertake pre-programmed survey missions. Among these AUVs, right now there are nearly 4,000 sensor probes called 'Argo floats' drifting through the deep sea in different regions, continually measuring conditions in the water and occasionally rising to the surface to transmit their findings via satellite so that oceanographers can study changes in the ocean.

Rather than eulogising the unknown that remains, we can reflect on how far we've come in our knowledge of the deep sea: from realising the varied terrain of the ocean floor and how it is formed, to appreciating the diversity of habitats that the deep sea contains and understanding how lots of species in those habi-tats overcome the trials of life. There's plenty still to explore and discoveries continue to come thick and fast, but there's also a lot that we already know about the deep sea – and this book is just a toe-dip into that.

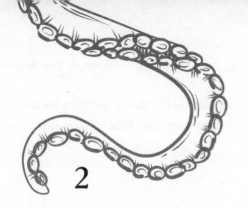

2

The Deep-Sea Floor Is Just as Varied as the World Above the Waves

The first glimpse of the ocean floor is one of the most exciting moments during a deep-sea dive, whether peering out of the portholes of a Human-Occupied Vehicle or watching the live video feed from a Remotely Operated Vehicle. Having spent perhaps a couple of hours slowly sinking through the darkness of the ocean's interior, at last the seabed comes within reach of your vehicle's lights. The most striking impression is always how different it seems compared with the familiar terrain around us on land – it feels like the 'touchdown' moment of landing on another world.

The reason the deep-sea floor seems other-worldly is because it is shaped by different processes to those that sculpt the land. Much of the landscape where I live in the southern UK, for example, has been shaped by water flowing across it, with energetic streams carving gullies in hillsides and slowly meandering rivers dropping off sediments to create broad plains. But that's not the case when the whole landscape, if we can still call it that, is underwater. When lava erupts from undersea volcanoes, it solidifies almost straight away, quenched by cold seawater to build hills that look like piles of lumpy blobs. And the tiny skeletons of deceased plankton sink perpetually from above, gradually blanketing the seafloor in fine mud formed by their remains. It's very different from the view out of my window.

A further lasting impression from diving into the deep sea is how unique each different location is. Above the waves, we have a varied landscape that includes mountain ranges, river plains, and rolling hills – and the deep sea is just as varied. It's certainly not *all* 'great grey level plains of ooze', as Rudyard Kipling described the deep-sea floor in his 1893 poem 'The Deep-Sea Cables' – though some areas are just like that, and 'ooze' is the technical term we use for muddy deep-sea sediments. In other locations on the ocean floor, you could be traversing the rocky bottom of a volcanic rift, diving down the steep slopes of an underwater mountain, or flying along a twisting undersea canyon, to mention just a few of the many deep-sea features out there.

We can take a tour of different deep-sea environments by following how the ocean floor is formed and transformed. The interior of our planet is made up of several layers: an inner and outer core, surrounded by a fluid mantle that is about 2,900 kilometres thick, and wrapped in a much thinner rocky crust. The crust comes in two varieties: the bits that we live on are 'continental crust', which is typically about 60 kilometres thick. The ocean floor is 'oceanic crust', which is usually less than

12 kilometres thick but more dense than continental crust. Consequently, the denser oceanic crust tends to settle below the continental crust, so the continental crust juts up to form landmasses and the oceanic crust lies below sea level.

The crust is divided into huge tectonic plates, of which there are seven major ones and several minor ones, which drift around over millions of years on currents in the underlying fluid mantle. Some plates consist of areas of oceanic crust and continental crust – the North American plate, for example, carries the continent of North America along with oceanic crust that spans half of the North Atlantic. As the plates jostle about, their oceanic crust is continually being created and destroyed by geological processes taking place beneath the waves. Consequently, the ocean floor is actually younger than the ocean that covers it – although our planet has had oceans for much of its 4.5-billion-year history, most of its current oceanic crust is less than 200 million years old. In contrast, the continental crust on the plates is more permanent, with rocks in some places that are 4 billion years old. And it's the shorter but more dynamic 'life cycle' of the oceanic crust that produces the variety of features that we find on the deep-sea floor.

Oceanic crust is created at mid-ocean ridges, where two plates are being pulled apart by currents in the

Earth's mantle. Lava wells up to fill the gap between the plates, creating a ridge on the ocean floor. The lava that oozes out along the mid-ocean ridge solidifies to create a new seabed, which is rocky and rugged because it hasn't had time to become covered in sediments sinking from above. Although we give separate names to the mid-ocean ridge in different oceans, such as the Mid-Atlantic Ridge, they join up to form a continuous feature that snakes around the globe like the seam on a tennis ball. That global mid-ocean ridge is 65,000 kilometres long, and its crest is around 2,600 metres deep on average, which is typically 2,000 metres shallower than the ocean floor around it.

The slopes of the mid-ocean ridge stretch out for up to 1,000 kilometres on either side of it, giving them an overall incline of around 1 in 500, which we wouldn't notice if we were hiking up it. Along the crest of the ridge there's usually a rift valley of up to 25 kilometres across and typically a kilometre or two deep, where the plates of the crust are being pulled apart. Unlike the gradual outer slopes of the ridge, the walls of the inner rift valley are very steep, even vertical in places, and its floor is usually jumbled with piles of solidified lava, so it would be a very challenging feature to hike across if it were on land.

The new seafloor created at the mid-ocean ridge is slowly pulled away from it, at about the same rate that our fingernails grow, as its plate drifts on the currents in the mantle. The age of the oceanic crust therefore increases with distance from the mid-ocean ridge, and sediments gradually settle on its rocky surface from overlying ocean, hiding the twisted blobs of solidified lava beneath a smoother covering of mud. If we travel away from the crest of a mid-ocean ridge, its rocky outer slope becomes rolling abyssal hills, usually a few kilometres across and a couple of hundred metres high. Abyssal hills are the underlying undulations of the rocky seafloor, formed by pulses in the lava erupting at the mid-ocean ridge and draped with the sediments that rain down relentlessly from above. More than a third of the world's ocean floor is covered by this hilly undersea terrain.

Eventually, even the undulations of the abyssal hills end up buried beneath the layer of sediments settling from the ocean. If we continue to travel away from a mid-ocean ridge on to older ocean floor, the abyssal hills give way to smoother abyssal plains. These plains stretch out for hundreds or even thousands of kilometres at depths typically around 4,000 to 5,000 metres, and cover more than a quarter of the global ocean floor. The oceanic crust beneath the abyssal plains may be a hundred million years old since it formed at a mid-ocean ridge, in which time it may have accumu-lated a layer of mud up to a kilometre thick – these are indeed the 'great grey level plains of ooze' that Kipling mentioned in his deep-sea poem.

But the mudflats of the abyssal plains are occasionally punctuated by undersea mountains, known as seamounts, which represent yet another deep-sea environment. The mid-ocean ridge isn't the only place where there's volcanic activity in the deep sea, and sometimes volcanoes erupt in the middle of a drifting plate of oceanic crust, if it travels over a hotspot in the Earth's mantle below. Some undersea volcanoes reach the surface as they grow from erupting lava, creating islands such as Hawaii, but most remain hidden beneath the waves as seamounts after their volcanic eruptions cease.

There are more than 43,000 seamounts known world-wide, and some of them rival peaks, such as the Alps, on land. The Great Meteor Seamount, for example, is one of the largest seamounts in the North Atlantic, rising from the surrounding seafloor at more than 4,200 metres deep to a summit around 270 metres deep. Its height of around 4,000 metres is similar to Piz Bernina, tallest of the eastern Alps. The sides of seamounts are typically steep, sometimes having an overall gradient of 1 in 4, with sheer cliffs in some places. Such slopes are too steep for sediment to settle on them – it just slides away downhill – so seamounts are simply islands of rock protruding from the muddy abyssal plains.

Professor Jon Copley

As the plates of the crust move apart at the mid-ocean ridges, they also collide with each other at their other edges. Where two plates of oceanic crust collide, one slips beneath the other, down into the mantle where it melts away. Where a plate of oceanic crust runs into a block of continental crust, the lighter continental crust ends up on top, and the oceanic crust similarly slides down to be consumed in the mantle. The process of an oceanic plate sinking down into the mantle is known as subduction, and it creates another deep-sea environment: ocean trenches, where the seafloor becomes more than 6,000 metres deep. There are twenty-seven ocean trenches where plates are subducting around the world, and although trenches cover less than 3 per cent of the total area of the ocean floor, they contain 45 per cent of its overall depth range, with five trenches reaching depths greater than 10,000 metres.

Ocean trenches are usually more than 50 kilometres wide, so if you were standing at the top of one side you wouldn't be able to see the top of the other side, because it would be over the horizon. Their walls can be very steep in some places, but overall they have a more gentle slope of about 1 in 10. The bottom of a trench is usually filled with soft sediment, which funnels down into the centre of the trench as it sinks from the ocean above. Mud also tumbles down the sides of a trench, like an underwater avalanche, when the seafloor is shaken by undersea earthquakes, which are more common where the plates of the Earth's crust are colliding.

Beyond these diverse environments that form on oceanic crust between its creation at a mid-ocean ridge and destruction beneath an ocean trench, there are yet more deep-sea features where the edges of continental crust meet the ocean. Earth's landmasses are fringed with continental shelves where the sea is mostly less than 200 metres deep, and then surrounded by continental slopes – the edges of the blocks of continental crust where the seabed increases in depth to around 4,000 metres deep. The continental slopes are typically a few tens of kilometres wide, so the overall gradient of their slope is perhaps 1 in 10.

The continental slopes are scarred with underwater canyons, known as submarine canyons, which are typically just a few kilometres across, unlike larger ocean trenches. Each submarine canyon meanders for a few hundred kilometres down a continental slope, but if you joined all of them together worldwide, they would stretch for about 25,000 kilometres – more than halfway around the Earth – so they're another common feature of the deep-sea floor.

With ridges, rift valleys, hills, plains, mountains, trenches, slopes and canyons, the terrain of the deep-sea floor is just as rich as the world above the waves.

And you may have noticed how the descriptions of deep-sea features have been littered with qualifiers, such as 'typically' and 'usually', because the varied conditions on the ocean floor defy our attempts to make generalisations about it. And that variety of environments is also important for the diversity of life in the deep sea, which we will explore in the next chapter.

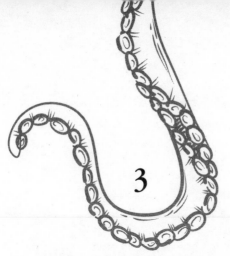

3

There Are Probably More than a Million Species of Animals in the Deep Sea

When HMS *Challenger* completed a pioneering round-the-world scientific voyage exploring the deep sea from 1872 to 1876, her hold was crammed with specimens of life forms dredged up from the ocean floor. Those specimens kept biologists busy for decades hence – they studied them in detail and described more than 4,700 new species. Many of the species discovered by the *Challenger* expedition were tiny plankton, described from their mineral skeletons that sank to form the mud of the ocean floor, but there were lots of new animals too. The species collected by *Challenger* included glow-in-the-dark sea pens (which are seabed-dwelling relatives of jellyfish) and plenty of deep-sea fishes, including the lizardfish *Bathysaurus mollis*, which lounges on the ocean floor with a reptilian-looking grin that fits its 'lizardfish' nickname.

Fast-forward from the *Challenger* expedition to today, and biologists are still routinely discovering new species of animals in the deep sea. In 2010, for example, my colleagues and I were exploring undersea hot springs, known as hydrothermal vents, at 2,400 metres deep in the Antarctic. All of the animals that we found thriving at those undersea hot springs – more than a dozen species, including a hairy-chested crab and a seven-armed starfish – were new to science, just at that particular spot in the deep sea.

Deep Sea: 10 Things You Should Know

The deep sea contains an astonishing diversity of animals, ranging in size and lifestyle, thanks to its variety of habitats. There are almost-microscopic crustaceans that drift throughout the ocean's interior alongside 13-metre-long giant squid that swim through it. Areas of the ocean floor that are covered by muddy sediments, such as the abyssal plains, are home to lots of forms that burrow into or crawl across it, from hair-thin nematode worms to sea cucumbers. Meanwhile, rocky areas, such as seamounts, and the steeper areas of continental slopes are often home to types of animals that attach themselves to a solid seafloor, such as deep-sea corals and sponges.

There are lots more habitats for different species beyond the variation between muddy and rocky areas of the seafloor too. The rift valley of the rocky mid-ocean ridge, for example, is dotted with hydrothermal vents, which are a further unique habitat for certain species. The whole ocean floor is also littered with the skeletons of animals whose carcasses have sunk from above, which are colonised by some animals that specialise in feeding on them. Some species create habitats for others too, such as deep-sea corals that live on seamounts and the steeper parts of continental slopes. The criss-crossing branches of those corals can build up over millennia into mounds tens of metres wide and high, which in turn provide shelter for hundreds of other species of animals, such as spindly-armed squat lobsters that nestle in the coral's lattice, and species of ragworms that burrow into the branches.

Although we certainly haven't yet seen all of the species that live in the deep sea, we can estimate how many are likely to live there by looking at the rate at which we find new ones. If we had discovered all the species that live in the deep sea, then no matter how much more we look, we wouldn't find any that we hadn't seen before. But if we haven't found all of them yet, then it should get harder to find new ones as we approach that goal. So we can look at the rate at which we are finding new species over time, and if we see a decline in that rate, we can extrapolate from that to predict how many undiscovered species may still be out there.

In the deep sea there's no sign yet of a decline in the rate at which we're finding new species. That might seem to throw a spanner in the works for estimating how many undiscovered species remain, but fortunately we can work around it. Species are like the thinnest branches on a tree of life, and each species-branch is the offshoot of a thicker branch in the tree, which gives rise to several species-branches. Biologists don't just identify different species, but also groups of species that represent those thicker branches in the tree of life. Each species belongs to a genus, which represents a group of closely related species. Lions and tigers, for example, have the scientific names *Panthera leo* and *Panthera tigris* because although they are different species, they are both members of the genus *Panthera*. In the same way, closely related genera – the plural of genus – then belong to the same family, and then there are further groupings, such as order, class, and phylum. Each of those groups represents a progressively thicker branch in the tree to which the thinner ones are attached.

Although the rate at which we're discovering new species isn't yet declining, we can look at the rate at which we're encountering new genera, families, orders, classes and phyla of animals, and we can see the rate of discovery is declining for some of those thicker branches in the tree of life. Finding a new phylum of animals, for example, is now extremely rare. There are about thirty phyla of animals currently living in the ocean, and different phyla typically have fundamental differences in how their bodies are organised – segmented worms, for example, belong to the phylum Annelida, while animals with exoskeletons and jointed limbs belong to the phylum Arthropoda. When a new phylum was described in 1998 – a new kind of parasitic animal found on the mouthparts of a lobster – it was a big deal in scientific circles. Because it's so rare to find a new phylum, we can be confident that we've found *almost* all of the different phyla that are out there.

The rate at which we're finding new classes, orders, and families of animals has begun to decline – and we're looking harder than we used to, with more expeditions currently exploring the deep sea than in the days of HMS *Challenger*. From those declining discovery rates, we can extrapolate how many classes, orders, and families of animals remain undiscovered. Then if we take the average number of species that typically belong to a family, order, and class, we can come up with a ballpark estimate for the total number of species that are out there. Doing all those sums gives us an estimate that there are around 7.77 million species of animals on Earth, and at least 2 million of them live in the ocean. Most of the ocean by area and volume is deep sea, and we know that the deep sea contains just as wide a range of habitats as the shallows, so it's a pretty safe bet that there are more than a million species of animals down there.

So far, scientists have described fewer than 200,000 species of deep-sea animals. But although we still have a very long way to go to know them all, we can learn a lot from those that we have identified. Finding out how these species thrive in the conditions they inhabit, for example, is giving us incredible insights to develop new medical treatments and even innovations for engineering.

One of my favourite examples of this is the scaly-foot snail *Chrysomallon squamiferum*, which lives at hydro-thermal vents between 1,700 and 2,900 metres deep in the Indian Ocean and whose species description my colleagues and I published in 2015. Unlike any other snail on land or under the sea, the fleshy foot of this species is covered with plates of metal minerals that form inside tiny pockets of its skin. The metal minerals are iron sulfides, and the snail creates the plates of them as part of a detoxification mechanism to cope with the conditions where it lives. The scaly-foot snail crawls around in warm water from the undersea hot springs that is rich in dissolved metals and hydrogen sulfide, which are toxic to most animals. But the snail gets rid of those toxins by turning them into the iron-sulfide scales covering its foot. And to create those waste-dump scales, the snail manages a feat that has so far eluded human engineers: it creates tiny crystals of iron sulfides at low temperatures.

Similar iron-sulfide crystals can be used to make more efficient solar panels, but such crystals aren't yet produced industrially, as the only way to make them has been at high temperatures in a laboratory using hazardous solvents. But the scaly-foot snail uses a molecule called myoglobin to create its iron-sulfide crystals while living in waters that are cooler than 25 degrees Celsius. Lots of animals, including humans, have myoglobin in their muscles, so it's not harmful and can be synthesised in a lab. Thanks to the scaly-foot snail, researchers have now shown how to make iron-sulfide crystals at lower temperatures using commercially available myoglobin, paving the way for easier production of those crystals for solar panels. So this small snail may in its own way contribute to the fight against climate change.

The scaly-foot snail is just one example of what we can learn from the diversity of life in the deep sea, and there are plenty more. Other deep-sea species contain compounds that have promising properties for developing new antibiotics, for example, and possibly new treatments for some types of cancer. The tremendous diversity of species in the deep sea is like a library of the ingenuity of nature – and that's a good reason to protect that biodiversity, so that we can continue to learn from it.

Discovering the species that thrive in the deep sea is also just the start of exploring life down there. Beyond finding out who lives in the deep sea, the further challenge is understanding what all those different species are doing – for example, finding out what they eat and how they reproduce. Exploring the lives of the million or so species of animals in the deep sea should keep us busy for a long time to come.

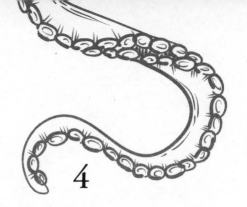

4

Pressure Is a Challenge for Deep-Sea Species – but Not in the Way that You Might Think

If you duck down to the bottom of a swimming pool, you may be familiar with feeling a squeeze in your ears that comes from the pressure of the water above you. That pressure increases relentlessly as you go deeper, at a rate of about one atmosphere of pressure for every 10 metres of water depth. That means where the deep sea begins at 200 metres deep, the water pressure is just over twenty times greater than the air pressure around you right now, and at the average ocean depth of around 3,500 metres, the conditions are more than 350 times normal atmospheric pressure.

The increase in pressure with depth is a challenge for air-breathing animals like us if we dive into the deep ocean without protecting our bodies from it. The deepest conditions that a human has survived with their body exposed to deep-sea pressures, in a simulated dive in a pressure chamber, were equivalent to a depth of 701 metres in the ocean, where the pressure is around seventy times that at the surface. The diver in that 1992 experiment, Theo Mavrostomos, had to breathe a special gas mixture of 49 per cent hydrogen, 50 per cent helium and 1 per cent oxygen at that simulated depth, and he spent a total of forty-three days shut inside a pressure chamber to acclimatise gradually to the high-pressure conditions and decompress slowly from them after the experiment was over.

Rather than exposing our bodies to high pressure, the Human-Occupied Vehicles that carry us into the deep ocean cocoon us at normal atmospheric pressure inside, so we can hop straight in and out of them without needing to acclimatise or decompress. Those vehicles need strong hulls to withstand the big difference in pressure between the deep sea outside and the normal surface conditions inside for their occupants. But how do deep-sea animals cope with the high-pressure conditions where they live, such as an amphipod crustacean 10 kilometres down in an ocean trench, where the pressure is a thousand times greater than at the surface? Unlike our deep-diving vehicles, the bodies of most deep-sea animals don't need to withstand a big difference in pressure between their surroundings and their insides. The main challenge of pressure for deep-sea species is what happens to molecules inside their cells, rather than withstanding pressure on their bodies.

The fish and invertebrate species that live permanently in the deep sea don't breathe air of course, and they extract the oxygen that they need from the seawater around them. This means that they don't usually have gas-filled spaces like our lungs inside them. Their bodies consist of the solid tissues of their organs and the liquids of their bodily fluids, which are much less compressible forms of matter – and that means that they don't have to withstand a difference in pressure between the conditions outside and inside their bodies.

If you drop a solid iron bar into the deep ocean, it doesn't collapse or implode, unlike sinking a sealed can of air. The solid bar remains intact because it is incompressible, and effectively the pressure inside it is the same as the pressure surrounding it. The same is true for most deep-sea animals because their bodies are only made of solids and liquids. You can test the compressibility of different states of matter for yourself: if you fill a syringe with air and hold your thumb over its nozzle, it's easy to compress the gas inside by pushing the plunger of the syringe. But try to do the same with a syringe full of water – you won't be able to move the plunger, no matter how hard you squeeze. And it's the same if you fill the syringe with something solid such as modelling clay. So with bodies made of incompressible solids and liquids, most deep-sea species don't have to physically resist the pressure of the deep sea around them, unlike our deep-diving vehicles with their air-filled spaces inside.

Instead, the big challenge of pressure for deep-sea life is at a molecular level. The cells of living organisms depend on enzymes, which control reactions in processes, such as metabolism and growth. Enzymes are protein molecules with complex three-dimensional structures – and it's vital that they have the right shape to work in catalysing the reactions of living processes. The protein molecule of an enzyme is built up from chains of amino acids, which usually spring into the right shape for the enzyme as they're being assembled inside cells. But under high-pressure conditions, water molecules get trapped on the chains of amino acids and prevent them from forming the correct shape for the enzyme.

Deep-sea animals have additional 'chaperone' molecules that help to pull the water off the chains of amino acids, so that they form into protein molecules with the right shape to work as enzymes. Fish and some crustaceans, such as shrimp and crabs, use a molecule called TMAO – which stands for trimethyl-amine oxide – as their chaperone molecule to overcome this problem with pressure. And the deeper they live, the more TMAO they have in their cells to help keep their enzymes in shape.

But having more TMAO can eventually become a problem in itself, because it also affects the amount of water inside cells. Too much TMAO can lead to cells containing more dissolved substances than seawater, which can prevent some ocean-dwelling species from keeping the right amount of water in their bodies for healthy physiology. This side effect of having more

TMAO may be the reason why there is a depth limit for some types of animals in the ocean. The deepest-known fish is a type of snailfish filmed at 8,336 metres deep in the Izu-Ogasawara Trench near Japan. By measuring how the amount of TMAO increases with depth in fish species, biologists predict that they should run into the problem of having too much TMAO by around 8,400 metres deep, which may explain why none have been seen at greater depths than that. So there is probably a fish-free zone, around 2 kilometres deep, between that limit and the bottom of the deepest ocean trenches. The other types of animals that live deeper than fish either use other chaperone molecules instead of TMAO, or have other ways of regulating the amount of water in their cells, so they don't run into the same limit.

Some species of fish run into a depth limit even sooner. There are more than 1,200 species of sharks, skates and rays, and collectively they are known as 'cartilaginous fishes' because their skeletons are made of cartilage rather than normal bones. The cartilaginous fishes use TMAO for another purpose, in addition to tackling the problem of pressure. Their cells contain lots of a substance called urea to control the amount of water in them, and urea also interferes with building protein molecules for enzymes. So the cartilaginous fishes have more TMAO in their cells than their bony fish cousins to deal with the problem of urea as well as the problem of pressure. The amount of TMAO in sharks, skates and rays increases with depth, but because their cells contain more of it than other fishes to cope with their urea, they reach the depth limit of too much TMAO sooner. The deepest-known cartilaginous fish is a Portuguese dogfish, *Centroscymnus coelolepis*, found at 3,675 metres deep – less than half the depth of the deepest-known bony fish, and consequently there are no sharks lurking in the deep ocean trenches.

Other animals use different 'chaperone' molecules, such as the amino acid proline, instead of TMAO to keep their enzymes in shape, and biologists are still exploring the depth limits of different types of animals. The deepest-known squid or octopus is a species of 'Dumbo' octopus – so-named because they can swim using two fins that look like elephant ears – filmed at 6,957 metres down in the Java Trench, and the current depth record for a prawn is 7,703 metres in the Japan Trench. But jellyfish have been seen at 10,000 metres deep, and sea anemones spotted even deeper at 10,900 metres.

It's worth noting that there are some air-breathing animals like us that do manage to dive into the deep sea, typically to forage for prey. Emperor penguins can dive to more than 500 metres deep, making them the champion divers of the birds. Leatherback turtles are one of the deepest-diving reptile species, some-times plunging to more than 1,200 metres deep in search of deep-living jellyfish. Among the seals, the hooded seal can dive to more than 1,000 metres deep, and the elephant seal can reach 2,000 metres deep. Sperm whales often dive between 1,000 and 2,000 metres deep to feed on deep-sea squid, and the current record for the deepest-diving whale is a Cuvier's beaked whale that reached 2,992 metres deep while wearing a recording tag in 2011. In most cases, these deep-diving air-breathers collapse their lungs during dives, rather than trying to keep them inflated against the potentially crushing pressure of the deep. And instead of carrying oxygen in their lungs to sustain them during their dives, they store oxygen in their bodies, attached to haemoglobin molecules in their blood and a similar molecule called myoglobin in their muscles.

For some types of animal, pressure presents even more problems than keeping enzymes in shape. The amphipod crustacean *Hirondellea gigas* is one of the species that lives at the deepest place on Earth – the Challenger Deep of the Mariana Trench, which is around 10,925 metres deep. Amphipods have an exoskeleton that contains the mineral calcite, which makes the exoskeleton rigid so that their muscles can attach to it and move their limbs. But calcite dissolves in seawater under the high-pressure conditions of the very deep ocean, which would make the trench-dwelling amphipod's exoskeleton floppy and useless for moving its limbs to swim and handle its food. Unlike shallower-living amphipods, *Hirondellea gigas* secretes a protective gel all over its exoskeleton to keep the calcite in it from dissolving away, rather like waxing a car. They're another reminder that although the deep sea may seem brutal to species like ours, it's just home to the animals that have adapted to its conditions.

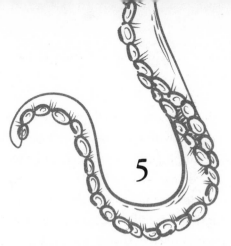

5

Food Is Scarce in the Deep Sea – Except Where it Isn't

The fangtooth fish *Anoplogaster cornuta* cruises through the deep sea at depths of between 500 and 2,000 metres and has some of the largest teeth of any vertebrate animal in proportion to its body size. The fangs that give the fish its name are so long that it can't close its mouth, and the fangtooth is one of several deep-sea fishes with mouths that bristle with teeth that look like cutlasses to tackle any prey that they encounter. But while it may appear scary to us in close-up, the fangtooth's body is about the size of a soft-drinks can, rather than it being a deep-sea monster of our imagination.

Food is often scarce in the deep ocean, and many deep-sea species have adaptations to make a meal out of anything they find. Some animals in the deep sea have nightmarish teeth and jaws like those of the fangtooth, but many do not, and other animals have evolved ways of extracting every last scrap of nutrition from whatever sinks to the ocean floor. The menu for deep-sea diners therefore is not just a diet of desperation, but also one of ingenuity as food becomes more scarce the deeper you go. But there are also some places in the deep sea where food is plentiful, thanks to microbes that can grow far beyond the reach of sunlight, which may give us a glimpse of how life could thrive elsewhere in the cosmos.

In the inner space of the ocean's interior, where food becomes more scarce, there are more than a hundred species of dragonfishes that have gaping jaws capable of swallowing prey almost as large as themselves. The necks of dragonfishes have a modified joint that allows their mouths to open up to 120-degrees to chomp larger animals. But cramming larger morsels into their mouths is only part of the challenge, and lots of deep-sea fishes also have elastic stomachs that can expand to accommodate such meals. The black swallower fish *Chiasmodon niger*, for example, was described as a species in 1864 from a specimen whose stomach contained the folded-up body of another fish nearly twice its own length.

In the eastern Pacific, the Humboldt squid *Dosidicus gigas* is one of the most voracious midwater predators at depths between 200 and 700 metres. Humboldts sometimes hunt in shoals of more than a thousand squid, jetting their 1.5 metre-long bodies through the water and slicing the flesh of their prey with hook-laden tentacles. They are also cannibals, attacking and consuming injured members of their own shoal. But while some deep-sea animals, such as Humboldt squid and dragonfishes, are active hunters, others are ambush predators, waiting for prey to pass close by or luring prey in. Where food is scarce, there may be advantages in ambushing your prey rather than expending energy chasing after it.

Giant siphonophores are one example of an ambush predator that drifts through the ocean depths. Their string-like bodies can be tens of metres long and are actually a chain of polyps living together as a colony – a floating city of individual animals. Some of the polyps dangle stinging tentacles into the water to catch food for the colony, creating a curtain of death for small crustaceans and fish that blunder into them. Meanwhile, down on the ocean floor at seamounts and mid-ocean ridges, there are at least 140 species of sponges that have eschewed their usual filter-feeding lifestyle and become carnivorous ambush predators, with sharp spines that skewer small crustaceans.

Most food chains in the ocean start in surface waters, where sunlight provides energy for tiny drifting algae to grow through the process of photosynthesis. A myriad of small animals, such as krill, graze those algae and are eaten by larger animals, such as fish or even ocean giants, such as the blue whale. At each step in these food chains, scraps of leftovers from messy eating, and the excrement of diners, and eventually their dead bodies sink into the deep sea below, providing food for its inhabitants. This detritus forms loose clumps poetically known as 'marine snow', which sinks slowly throughout the deep ocean.

Lots of deep-sea animals feed on marine snow instead of being predators, and the vampire squid

Vampyroteuthis infernalis is one example. Unlike their hunter cousins, the vampire squid avoids energetic pursuits and feeds by stretching out two of its ten arms that are modified into thin, sticky filaments to catch the softly sinking detritus. When the vampire squid reels those arms back in, it wipes off the marine snow to eat. This provides less of a meal than hunting prey, but as the vampire squid just hangs out in the ocean and has the lowest metabolic rate of any squid, it's enough for them. Vampire squid tend to live in a layer of the ocean where oxygen is scarce, which they can tolerate but predators perhaps cannot, and this may help them avoid becoming a meal themselves while they bob about, fishing for marine snow.

For animals living on the deep-sea floor, marine snow can be a steady source of food, though perhaps a scant one as much of the nutrition it contains has been consumed on its journey down through the ocean. Sea cucumbers, which are related to starfish but typically have sausage-shaped bodies, are commonly seen animals on abyssal plains, ploughing their way through the marine snow that has settled on the seabed. The bodies of deep-living sea cucumbers are often translucent with a pinkish or purple tinge, and you can see the loops of their guts inside them, packed with the marine snow that they are digesting to extract the remnants of food that it contains. As well as crawling slowly across the seafloor and swallowing marine snow as they go, some species of sea cucumber can also swim gently from one patch of marine snow to another – and they usually defecate just before take-off to lighten their bodies.

Other animals on the seafloor catch the sinking marine snow as it settles from above or drifts past them in ocean currents. Deep-sea feather stars, for example, perch on rocks and stretch out their feathery arms to intercept marine snow drifting past. Feather stars are also related to sea stars, and like sea stars their arms are lined with tiny tube feet. A feather star's arms are sticky to catch marine snow, which its tube feet then pass along the arm to the animal's mouth. If disturbed by a potential predator, feather stars can swim away to find another perch, waving their feathery arms to propel themselves through the water before stretching them out like a parachute for a gentle landing, and grabbing on to a new rocky perch with grapple-like appendages on the underside of their bodies.

Not all the food that sinks to the ocean floor is tiny particles of marine snow, however. Occasionally larger parcels of food sink to the seabed, such as the carcasses of dead fish from the ocean above. Lots of bottom-dwelling animals are scavengers, cruising the seabed to find these richer 'foodfalls', and often using an underwater sense of smell to home in on them.

Sometimes larger foodfalls contain nutrition that doesn't get consumed on the way to the ocean floor because it is in a form that most organisms can't use. Each year more than 3 million tonnes of wood are naturally washed out to sea from forested coastal areas, and much of it eventually sinks to the ocean floor as 'woodfalls'. The cellulose and lignin in wood are potential food, but are hard to digest unless you have the right enzymes to break down those molecules. There are more than fifty species of wood-eating clams in the deep sea that burrow into sunken wood and have bacteria inside their guts that produce the enzymes to digest it. These wood-boring clams can turn a block of wood into a hollow honeycomb of burrows within a few months, and their appetite for wood is one of the reasons why wooden shipwrecks are often poorly preserved on the deep seafloor.

Bones are another form of locked-up food in the deep sea. Deep-sea scavengers quickly strip the flesh off the sunken carcasses of animals, such as fishes and whales, but leave their skeletons exposed on the seafloor. There is still potential food inside those bones, caged within the inedible minerals of the bone itself. Bone-eating 'zombie' worms, of which there are at least twenty-five species, quickly colonise bones on the seafloor and secrete an acid that dissolves the mineral part of the bone, unlocking the food within. It may be the fate of all skeletons in the deep sea, including those of unfortunate mariners, to be eventually consumed by these bone-eating worms. Very little goes to waste in the deep sea – the ingenuity of nature ensures that whatever can be eaten often does get eaten.

But there are some places in the deep sea where there is enough food for an astonishing abundance of animals, in contrast to the otherwise sparse life on the ocean floor. Pulsating piles of deep-sea snails and mounds of white-bodied crabs are just some of the animals that thrive around hydrothermal vents, and how such an abundance of life can thrive in the deep sea was initially a mystery, until biologists figured out its secret.

The hot water that gushes out of hydrothermal vents on the ocean floor is rich in dissolved minerals, such as hydrogen sulfide, which some microbes can use as an energy source to grow. The process is very similar to photosynthesis, but powered by chemical energy instead of sunlight, and therefore known as chemosynthesis. Rather than food chains starting in sunlit surface waters far above, microbes produce food locally at hydrothermal vents – the answer to the puzzle of how such a lot of life thrives at these oasis-like places in the deep.

Animals at deep-sea vents often live in partnerships with those chemosynthetic microbes, in some cases culturing them in organs inside their bodies to consume as they grow, or in other cases gardening them on the outside of their bodies to scrape off and eat. The scaly-foot snail *Chrysomallon squamiferum* is one of the former, growing chemosynthetic bacteria inside a bag-like organ attached to its oesophagus. And the Hoff crab *Kiwa tyleri* – nicknamed in honour of the hairy-chested actor David Hasslehoff – is an example of the latter, combing bacteria off its hairy chest for its dinner. Both live in seething stacks of their species at hydrothermal vents, jostling to bathe in the vent waters to nourish their bacteria.

But hydrothermal vents are not the only places in the deep sea where chemosynthesis provides food for lush colonies of animals. At cold seeps, the same chemical compounds needed for chemosynthesis flow out of the seabed, although those seeping fluids are not hot like the gushing waters of the vents. There are lots of different types of cold seeps, such as brine pools and mud volcanoes, driven by different geological processes, and they are home to similar colonies of deep-sea animals to those found at hydrothermal vents, such as meadows of tubeworms and carpets of mussels that have chemosynthetic bacteria living inside them.

Chemosynthesis also occurs at woodfalls when bacteria break down the copious excrement of wood-eating clams inside their burrows. Breaking down that organic matter in the low-oxygen conditions of the burrows releases hydrogen sulfide, which in turn provides energy for chemosynthetic microbes. And a similar process takes place inside the large bones of whale skeletons on the seafloor when bacteria break down fats stored in the whale bones, again releasing hydrogen sulfide. In both cases, the flow of hydrogen sulfide from the wood or whale bone can support animals that live in partnership with chemosynthetic microbes, such as some species of deep-sea mussels that colonise woodfalls and whalefalls.

Chemosynthesis amazed me as a student, revealing how life can be supported without sunlight as an energy source, and has sparked my fascination since with exploring the places where it occurs in the deep sea. But in addition to chemosynthesis, we now know that some deep-sea microbes can grow at hydrothermal vents through a process known as electrosynthesis, harnessing the energy of tiny electrical currents created by reactions between rocks and seawater. Exploring the deep sea doesn't just teach us that 'life finds a way', to borrow a quote from *Jurassic Park*, but that actually, life finds lots of ways to thrive, which may be a useful lesson as we peer out into the cosmos to ponder whether and how life could exist beyond our blue planet.

6

Finding a Mate Can Be Tricky in the Deep Sea – but Finding a Home Seems Easy

All animals face similar trials in life: searching for food, avoiding being eaten, finding a mate and rearing their offspring, and then those offspring finding a home. And just as deep-sea animals overcome the challenge of finding food in lots of different ways, the same is true for those other challenges.

Populations of deep-sea animals often become sparse where food is scarce in the deep sea, which can make it difficult to meet a member of the opposite sex for reproduction. As a result, some deep-sea animals take an opportunistic, 'have-a-go' approach to mating. In several species of deep-sea squids and octopuses, for example, males try to mate with any potential partner that they meet, regardless of their sex or even their species.

Mating in squids involves the male passing a spear-like packet of sperm down a groove in one of their arms to stick on to a female's body, ready to release its contents when she produces her eggs. But male squid collected in nets from the deep sometimes have sperm spears stuck on their bodies too, in places where the jabs can't have been self-inflicted, indicating attempted mating by another male. Attempted inter-species mating has also been observed: in 1994 scientists diving in a Human-Occupied Vehicle filmed two male octopuses of different species trying to mate with each other, 2,500 metres down on the ocean floor of the eastern Pacific Ocean.

As an alternative to indiscriminate mating, some deep-sea animals stay with a partner once they've met them. The sea cucumber *Paroriza pallens* looks like a mouldy banana and spends its adult life crawling across the abyssal plains, leaving a track that can be seen in photographs of the seafloor. Sometimes the single track of a *Paroriza* meets another, and then the two trails continue side-by-side like a railway line. At the end of those tell-tale twin tracks there's a pair of *Paroriza*, now wandering across the abyssal plain together.

Paroriza sea cucumbers are hermaphrodites that develop male and female sex organs at the same time, but they can't self-fertilise. Instead, the sperm produced by each partner fertilises the eggs produced by the other partner. Staying together means that one partner is always available to fertilise the other's eggs whenever they produce them – and the story of their encounter and subsequent fidelity is recorded in their trails on the soft mud of the abyssal plain.

When it comes to keeping a male handy for fertilising eggs, several deep-sea animals have evolved a more extreme solution. Wood-eating clams, bone-eating 'zombie' worms, and some species of anglerfishes have tiny males that attach themselves to a female once they've found her, acting as standby 'accessory males' to fertilise the female's eggs when needed. In some species of bone-eating worms, for example, one female can have a harem of a dozen or more males, each about a hundred times smaller than the female, hanging on to her with microscopic hooks.

About two dozen species of anglerfish that live in the deep sea also have accessory males to varying degrees. In some species, the smaller male attaches temporarily to a female, but he can swim off and hook up with another female. In other species, however, the male fuses his mouth on to the female's body in a kiss that lasts the rest of his life. The male's blood supply joins up with hers through his lips, and he can no longer leave her or feed himself: he becomes a parasitic provider of sperm on-tap, nourished by the female through their shared circulation as she continues to feed. In some species, only one male forms this life-long union with a female, but in others, one female can have several accessory males dangling off her at any one time.

But there's a complication in such a permanent pairing. Fish have an immune system with two main parts like ours. The 'innate' immune system produces general defences to fight off infections, while the 'adaptive' immune system recognises and attacks any 'foreign' substances, including cells that are genetically different to the rest of the body. That adaptive immune system is great for tackling would-be invaders, such as disease-causing bacteria, but is a problem when sharing a blood supply with a partner. If we were to join our blood supply to that of another person, our adaptive immune systems would attack each other through the shared circulation, unless we were closely related genetically. It's similar to how organ transplants have to be carefully chosen and treated to reduce the risk of being rejected – so how do these deep-sea anglerfish avoid rejecting their partner in the same way?

The anglerfish species with males that attach permanently to females lack several genes that enable their adaptive immune system to recognise cells that are not their own. This means that their adaptive immune systems don't attack each other when they pair up – but it also implies that they may be less able to fight off infections than other fish. It's possible, however, that the innate immune system of those anglerfish species may compensate by producing better general defences to fight off infection. Further research into how those anglerfish manage without a normal adaptive immune system might even reveal new ways to treat infections in humans.

Nurturing the fruits of all these unions is the next trial of life, and it's just as varied in deep-sea animals as it is among species on land. Some deep-sea species just release their fertilised eggs into the ocean to develop without any further care, but others look after their brood until they hatch. The icefish *Neopagetopsis ionah*, for example, makes a nest of rocky debris on an otherwise muddy seafloor, which helps to keep its eggs bathed in well-oxygenated seawater. In 2021, a seafloor survey came across an astonishing colony of icefish nests at around 500 metres deep in the Weddell Sea of the Antarctic, in a spot where ocean currents bring slightly warmer water to the seabed than the surrounding area. At that location there are an estimated sixty million icefish nests packed into about 240 square kilometres of seabed, which is almost the size of inner London. Each nest is about three-quarters of a metre across and most of those surveyed contained an icefish guarding around 1,700 eggs. It's the largest known breeding colony of any fish, and the slightly warmer water at that location may speed up the development of the embryos inside the eggs, making it such an attractive place for the icefish to nest there.

At hydrothermal vents near the South Sandwich Islands, Hoff crabs bask in mineral-rich waters, growing bacteria on their hairy chests to eat. Males and females mingle in huge piles near the vents, and after mating the female Hoff crabs tuck their developing embryos under their curved lobster-like tails. But the piles of jostling crabs at the vents are not a good place to rear their offspring, as the minerals in the vent waters are

toxic for a developing embryo. The females will therefore traipse through a gauntlet of predatory anemones
and starfish to brood their embryos tens of metres away
from the vents. Out there, while they wait for their
eggs to hatch, the females go without food and their
bodies start to waste away because they're no longer
bathed in the mineral-rich vent water that nourishes
the bacteria that they eat. The males, meanwhile, stay
close to the vents and continue to garden bacteria on
their bodies, stuffing their faces and becoming about
three times the size of the females as a result.

The trophy for the most dedicated parent in the deep
sea has to go to the octopus *Grandeledone boreopacifica*.
This species sticks eggs on to rocky outcrops on the
seafloor, and then the mother keeps watch over them,
no longer feeding herself and dying after they hatch. In
2007, marine biologists came across a female octopus
guarding a batch of 160 eggs at 1,400 metres deep in
Monterey Bay. Identifiable by marks on her body, she
was still keeping vigil each time the biologists returned
to that spot over the next four-and-a-half years – the
longest egg-brooding known for any animal in the sea
or on land. The common octopus in shallow water,
in contrast, broods eggs for just four to eight weeks.

Once they hatch, the offspring of deep-sea animals
typically undergo a larval stage in their life cycle,
which sometimes resembles the adult animal or may

look very different to its grown-up form. Newly hatched octopuses, for example, usually look like miniature octopuses, but the Hoff crab has a larva that looks more like a tiny shrimp than a crab. These larval stages often disperse on ocean currents before growing into adults, which enables them to overcome the other trial of finding a home.

Some deep-sea habitats are temporary – each wood fall or whale fall on the ocean floor is eventually consumed by the animals that feed on it, for example, and the flow of mineral-rich water at a hydrothermal vent or cold seep gradually fades out as its plumbing gets clogged up with mineral deposits. But new patches of these habitats are also being created on the ocean floor as more wood or another whale carcass sinks to the seabed, or a new vent or seep springs up. The species that live in these habitats must be able to disperse to new patches over time, otherwise they would die out.

Some animals can't relocate as adults – a tubeworm at a hydrothermal vent, for example, lives inside a tube glued to the rocky seafloor. Even for animals that can crawl or swim, it's usually too far for them to reach another patch of habitat, which may be tens or hundreds of kilometres away. It tends then to be the larval stage of their life cycle that heads out into the dark yonder to find a new home.

Some species have larvae that can't feed but are sustained by an internal store of yolk as they drift on ocean currents. In the typically cold water of the deep sea, the metabolism of the larva may tick over slowly, eking out the energy in its yolk store. The larva of the vent tubeworm *Riftia pachyptila*, for example, can survive for about thirty-eight days before its reserves run out. During that time, ocean currents can carry it up to a hundred kilometres, passing over several clusters of hydrothermal vents, which are only tens of kilometres apart where that species lives in the eastern Pacific.

Some species have larval stages that can feed, which enables them to survive much longer and travel much further. The vent shrimp *Rimicaris exoculata* has a larva that feeds on marine snow, and they may spend years drifting through the ocean. Colonies of the shrimp are genetically similar at hydrothermal vents along 7,000 kilometres of the Mid-Atlantic Ridge, (the same distance between London and Miami), indicating that their larvae are dispersing between the vents over that huge range.

Whenever we as scientists put a block of wood or a bone on the ocean floor to find out what colonises it, animals, such as wood-boring clams or bone-eating worms, typically arrive and start to grow into adults within just a few weeks. So the deep sea must be fairly awash with their larvae, sloshing about on ocean currents to find a new home. Although it may seem like a challenge to us, deep-sea species appear to be pretty adept at getting around. Exactly how a drifting larva detects a patch of suitable habitat on the seafloor is still a mystery, but whatever they are doing clearly works to sustain their populations in space and time.

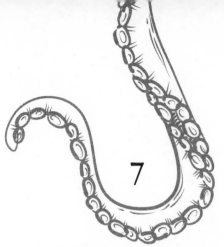

7

The Deep Sea is a Dark Place, but There Are Lights – and Plenty of Eyes to See Them

Sunlight fades away when you descend into the deep sea in a minisub. As you leave the grip of the waves at the surface, the water around you starts to look bluer and bluer, becoming a deeper blue than you can imagine. Then even that deep blue fades out before you are a couple of hundred metres deep, and it feels like you are wrapped in blackness, dropping through a dark space that goes on to the ocean floor thousands of metres below.

But if you press your face up against a porthole – and cup your hands around your eyes to block out the glow from the sub's instruments around you – you become aware of flashes and squirts of light in the inky blackness outside. Those lights seem to streak up past you, as your sub descends past the animals that produce them.

So although the deep sea is a dark place, it is decorated with lights made by its inhabitants, whose displays are known as bioluminescence. And the ocean floor itself is dotted with other mysterious sources of light. Consequently, many deep-sea animals have eyes despite living in the dark, and they use their lights and eyes for lots of different purposes.

Although it's too faint for our eyes to see, sunlight can reach down to a thousand metres deep before it is completely quenched by the ocean, if you are in the clearest offshore waters at the brightest noon. This upper reach of the deep sea is nicknamed 'the twilight zone' because there is still some faint light coming from the sunlit world above.

Life in the twilight zone involves a game of hide-and-seek between predators and prey. Any animal living in the faint downwelling sunlight potentially casts a shadow beneath it, and many animals in the twilight zone have very sensitive upward-looking eyes to detect the shadows of potential prey. The eyes of the glasshead barreleye fish *Rhynchohyalus natalensis* are some of the strangest, with long lenses – hence the 'barreleye' part of its name – that look upwards through the transparent top of its head. But as well as looking out for shadows of prey above, the glasshead barreleye can keep watch for potential predators below. This fish's eyes also contain natural mirrors that reflect the view from two smaller eyeholes on the underside of its head. These 'diverticular' eyes – which have evolved in a couple of different types of deep-sea fishes – peer upwards and peep downwards at the same time.

More than 90 per cent of the animals living in the twilight zone are bioluminescent, and many of them use their lights for a camouflage trick called counter-illumination. For example, deep-sea shrimps that belong to a group of species called the Oplophoridae have light-producing organs dotted around their bodies, and particularly on their undersides. These light-making organs shine out with light that matches the faint sunlight coming from above. This breaks up the silhouette of the shrimps in the downwelling light, so their outline seems to disappear to any predator looking up from below. But the brightness of the faint sunlight surrounding the shrimps can change, especially if they swim up or down in twilight zone. So the light-producing organs of the Oplophoridae shrimps are also light-sensors, monitoring the light around them to match it with their displays and keep up their vanishing trick.

Another way to fool the eyes of potential predators is to look like something else. Some species of deep-sea eelpout fish curl up their bodies into circles or C-shapes when predators pass nearby. They hang motionless in the water, instead of continuing their usual sinuous swimming, and may thereby resemble unappetising jellyfish to be ignored. But perhaps the ultimate way to hide from the eyes of predators is to become invisible, and some deep-sea animals come close to doing that. There are several species of 'glass' squid, for example, that have see-through bodies as an alternative way to avoid casting shadows in the twilight zone or showing up in the bioluminescent headlights used by some deep-sea hunters.

A few deep-sea predators use transparent tricks too.

Some dragonfishes have teeth made out of the same mineral as our own pearly whites, but with the mineral crystals rearranged so that the dragonfish's teeth are see-through. These transparent teeth, which are just as strong as ours and savagely sharp, don't gleam in any light from their prey as the dragonfish closes in with a wide-open mouth.

Beyond the twilight zone, we descend into the 'midnight zone', forever beyond the reach of the sun's rays. As there's no more light from above, there are no shadows for hide-and-seek here, but still plenty of bioluminescence and lots of eyes. Animals in both zones use lights to catch their food, and many are ambush predators, luring their prey with bioluminescent bait. The glowing-sucker octopus *Stauroteuthis syrtensis* for example has rows of suckers on its arms that produce light instead of being able to stick to things, and those lights attract small crustaceans to its mouth, where the rows of lights converge.

Other deep-sea dwellers are active hunters, using bioluminescent searchlights to find their prey in the darkness and chase them down. The stoplight loosejaw fish *Malacosteus niger* is one of the most remarkable of these hunters, with a tear-shaped organ below each eye that produces red light, giving it the 'stoplight' part of its name. Most deep-sea bioluminescence is blue or blue-green, because those wavelengths of light travel furthest through the water. The eyes of almost all the deep-sea animals studied so far can only see those blue or blue-green wavelengths and can't detect red light. But the stoplight loosejaw is an exception, because the retina of its eye contains a compound that boosts the colour range of its vision beyond the usual blue-green sensitivity of other deep-sea fishes. This means that the stoplight loosejaw can illuminate prey with its red searchlights without its victims being aware that they have been targeted.

Camouflage in the midnight zone involves blending in with the black background to avoid showing up in the searchlights of hunters. Quite a lot of midnight zone animals have red bodies, which may be camouflage because red appears black in the blue or blue-green light of most deep-sea bioluminescence, and red pigments may be easier to produce than more complex black pigments. But at least sixteen species of deep-sea fishes, belonging to seven different branches of the evolutionary tree, have ultra-black skin to hide from predators. Objects that appear black to us still reflect about 2 to 5 per cent of the light that falls on them, but the skin of those ultra-black deep-sea fishes reflects less than half a per cent of the light that falls on it – so they are almost as black as it's possible to get. They achieve their ultra-black look with structures in the skin called melanosomes that contain black pigment and are arranged to absorb as much light as possible.

Distracting predators with bioluminescent displays when threatened is an alternative to camouflage, as practised by the green bomber worm *Swima bombviridis*. This worm grows green bioluminescent gills that it can jettison as countermeasures to confuse attackers while the worm swims away into the darkness and eventually grows new gills. Meanwhile, other deep-sea animals can deter predators with bioluminescent warnings. The velvet-belly lanternshark *Etmopterus spinax* has spines on its back that make it an uncomfortable mouthful for predators, and it advertises those spines with light organs around them to warn off hunters.

Beyond the struggles between predators and prey, deep-sea animals also use bioluminescence to attract or recognise mates. Although our knowledge of this form of communication is limited in the dark depths, the different patterns of light-producing organs on males and females of several deep-sea species are a good indication of this use. In several species of lanternfishes, males have light-producing organs at their tails that can emit fast pulses of light, which may be signals to females and are unlike the continuous light from other organs that both sexes use for counter-illumination camouflage.

Down on the ocean floor, only around 20 per cent of the species are bioluminescent – a lower percentage than among the animals drifting and swimming in the mid-water zones. The horizon limits the distance that bottom-dwelling animals can see a bioluminescent display on the seafloor, compared with a light beaming out into the inner space of the ocean's interior. Nevertheless, some seafloor animals are bioluminescent, such as the scaleworm *Neopolynoe chondrocladiae*, which lives inside a carnivorous deep-sea sponge. The worm's bioluminescence shines through the basket-like fibres of the sponge's skeleton, and may help to attract small crustaceans that the sponge and the worm both feed on.

The remains of animals, such as fish and crustaceans, that sink to the seafloor may glow faintly with bioluminescence from bacteria that decompose them, and some deep-sea scavengers may be able to detect that glow, helping them to home in on the carcass after their sense of smell has brought them to its general vicinity. *Booralana tricarinata* is a species of isopod crustacean, similar to a woodlouse or pill bug, that scavenges on such sunken remains. Its compound eyes are very sensitive, but they have a very slow 'refresh rate': they only update the image for the brain about four times per second. So while the eyes of *Booralana* cannot track fast-moving prey or detect quick flashes of bioluminesence, they are great for guiding it towards the dim but steady glow of a rotting fish carcass on the seafloor.

With bioluminescence put to so many uses, and with so many types of eyes to see it, the deep sea is not a realm of complete darkness or largely inhabited by blind animals. And there are other non-bioluminescent sources of light on the ocean floor, which some animals can detect too. There's a faint glow where hot water gushes out of the mineral spires of deep-sea hydrothermal vents. Some of that glow comes from the sheer heat of the vent water, which can be more than 400 degrees Celsius, but some of it probably comes from chemical reactions as the mineral-rich vent water mixes with normal seawater.

The vent light is too faint for a human eye to see, but it can be recorded with a sensitive camera. Some species of shrimp that thrive around hydrothermal vents have a light-sensing organ on their backs – a modified eye that has become a sheet of light-sensitive cells, lacking a lens to form an image but capable of detecting the dim flicker of the vents. These light-sensors may help the shrimps to navigate around the mineral spires of the vents. And the light of those vents even powers some microbial life. There is a strain of green sulfur bacteria – so-called because they contain the green chlorophyll pigment – that grows on vent spires and uses the faint glow as an energy source to turn carbon dioxide in the hot vent water into sugar molecules for sustenance. So yet again, life finds a way: photosynthesis that uses geolight instead of sunlight in the deep sea.

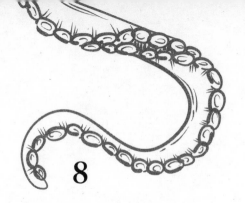

8

Deep-Sea Animals Use Lots of Senses Beyond Vision to Overcome the Trials of Life

Consider the life of a female Hoff crab at a hydro-thermal vent: she crawls around the mineral spires of the vent without blundering into scalding-hot vent water that would cook her, while also not straying too far away from the mineral-rich flow that nourishes the bacteria that she grows on her chest to eat. She manages to find a partner for mating and migrates away from the vent area to brood her offspring – and then finds her way back to the vent to feed and reproduce again. Somehow she does all this without being able to see, as Hoff crabs are one of the species in the deep sea that doesn't have any eyes.

Even for those species that do have eyes, light from their own bioluminescent organs or those of their prey doesn't travel very far through seawater before it dims, so deep-sea animals use other senses to find their food and communicate with each other over greater distances than they can see. As a result, the deep sea isn't only punctuated with the twinkling lights of bioluminescence – it's also filled with smells and sounds.

Lots of animals that scavenge for food on the seafloor use an underwater sense of smell to find their meals. A fish carcass that has settled on the seabed, for example, gives off an odour plume that wafts away on ocean currents. Grenadier fish patrol across the flow of ocean currents to sniff out any foodfalls that have landed 'upwind' of them – and then they turn to swim up-current if they detect one, following their noses to it.

Underwater smells are also sometimes important for finding a mate. The males of some deep-sea anglerfish have a well-developed olfactory (smell) system, so it's likely that females of those species release a phero-mone to attract their mates. There's probably a lot of smell-signalling going on during courtship in deep-sea species, but often we can only guess when it may be happening from differences between the sensory organs of males and females, because collecting and identifying actual pheromones is incredibly tricky.

The mineral-rich water gushing from hydrothermal vents is another kind of odour that some deep-sea species can detect. The shrimp *Rimicaris exoculata* that swarms around vents on the Mid-Atlantic Ridge has two pairs of antennae that can detect hydrogen sulfide – which smells like rotten eggs to us – that is dissolved in vent water. The vent shrimp need to find a spot near the vents where they are bathed in sulfide-laden water to cultivate bacteria on their bodies to eat. And like the Hoff crab, they also need to avoid blundering into the hottest vent waters, which can reach 400 degrees Celsius. Their sulfide-sniffing antennae may help them to achieve this – the Hoff crab may have a similar ability, though we haven't figured it out yet for that species.

As well as a sense of smell, some deep-sea animals have a sense of touch that works over a distance. Deep-sea fishes have sensory organs arranged in lines running down their bodies, known as the lateral line system, that can detect disturbances in the water around them. Those disturbances could be from scavengers scrapping over a nearby foodfall on the seafloor, or the evasive manoeuvres of prey, or the fast approach of a predator – so there are lots of advantages to having this sense of touch that reaches out into their surroundings. And among deep-sea sharks, the lateral line system includes organs that can detect tiny electrical fields produced by living animals, which enables some species to detect prey buried in the sediments of the seafloor.

When it comes to detecting sound, deep-sea fishes have ears buried inside their heads that include three semi-circular canal structures like those in our inner ears. Their ears also have structures called otolith organs, which contain small mineral deposits that stimulate sensitive hairs when they're moved by vibrations from sounds passing through seawater. The bony-eared assfish *Acanthonus armatus* is a deep-sea species that has proportionally the largest semi-circular canals of any fish and particularly heavy mineral deposits in its otolith organs. As a result, its ears are very sensitive to low-frequency sounds, which travel furthest underwater. In some other deep-sea fish, such as the blue hake *Antimora rostrata*, their ears are connected to their swim bladder – an organ that some fishes have to control their buoyancy – which can also make their hearing more sensitive, possibly to detect any noisy commotion made by fellow scavengers at a nearby foodfall.

Some deep-sea fishes have muscles attached to their swim bladder that enable them to produce sound by drumming on it. But recognising the sounds of deep-sea fishes in recordings from underwater microphones is difficult, because it can be hard to isolate one sound and identify the particular fish that made it. Some deep-sea species from less than a thousand metres deep can be kept in aquaculture tanks, however, so we can hear their sounds. A couple of species of cusk eels, for example, make growling noises, while sablefish produce rasps. As there are differences in the swim bladder muscles between males and females of these species, it's likely that such sounds play a role in their courtship.

Toothed whales are the masters of sound production in the deep sea, in terms of volume and control. All the species of whales, dolphins and porpoises can be divided into two groups: baleen whales and toothed whales. The baleen whales, which include humpbacks and blue whales, harvest small animals, such as krill, from the water and don't tend to dive particularly deep. But the toothed whales, which also includes dolphins and porpoises, sometimes dive much deeper to hunt for fish and squid. Sperm whales are toothed whales that routinely dive more than a thousand metres deep, for example, and the Cuvier's beaked whale that reached 2,992 metres deep while wearing a depth-recording tag is also a species of toothed whale.

Baleen and toothed whales all produce calls to communicate with each other, from the whistles of dolphins to the songs of humpbacks, but toothed whales also produce clicks and buzzes to find their prey by echolocation. To make their echolocation sounds during dives, toothed whales store air in nasal cavities and pass that air over 'phonic lips' that are similar to our vocal chords, but in their nose rather than in their throats. The vibrations of the phonic lips are then focused by a structure called the melon inside their head, creating pulses of sound that beam out into the water to bounce off their prey.

Toothed whales use different types of voice, known as vocal registers, to produce different types of sound. For their communication calls, they use normal and falsetto registers, which are similar to our usual speaking voice and high-pitched singing like the

Bee Gees. But for their echolocation clicks, they use a register called 'vocal fry': a low-pitched gravelly noise, like the sound of frying bacon – sometimes used by people in 'errs' when thinking about what to say or clearing our voice for speaking, or by some singers such as Leonard Cohen.

Using vocal fry instead of the higher-pitched registers allows toothed whales to generate sounds from very small volumes of air passing over their phonic lips, thereby making best use of the relatively small volume of air stored in their nasal cavities during dives. And the sounds from their vocal fry can be very loud – the echolocation clicks of sperm whales can reach 230 decibels, which puts them among the loudest noises produced by any animal on our planet. But they typically make their echolocation signals quieter as they close in on prey, turning down the volume when they are about a body-length away and switching from clicks into a more continuous buzz, which provides more detailed information about the exact position of their target before they suck it into their mouth. Although they are toothed whales, sperm whales perhaps don't use their teeth very much, as the bodies of prey in their stomachs seldom have tooth marks on them, indicating that they were taken by a swift swoop-and-swallow.

Beyond the sounds made by animals in the deep sea, there's background noise from other natural sources, which some species might use to navigate or find a home. Volcanic activity and earthquakes on the ocean floor produce rumbles that we can detect with networks of underwater microphones, for example, and the ears of some deep-sea fishes are sensitive to such low-frequency sounds, which might help to guide the migrations of some species across the ocean floor. Hydrothermal vents also make a noise, rather like the low thrum of an aircraft engine during flight, which should be detectable to the hearing of some of the animals that live around them. These background sounds might be part of the puzzle of how animals find a home in the deep sea, perhaps helping the larvae of some species to determine where to settle while they are drifting about on ocean currents. But the sounds of human activities, from the traffic noise of shipping to the underwater explosions used to survey for offshore oil and gas, now also permeate the deep sea – and we don't yet understand all the ways that our noise could be disrupting life down there.

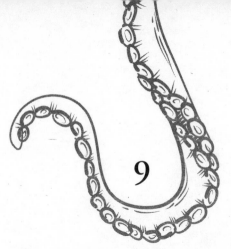

9

There Are Days, Seasons and Tides in the Deep Sea – and Life Responds to those Rhythms

The annual journey of our tilted planet around its star, which gives us shorter and longer days in different seasons, might seem irrelevant to inhabitants of the deep sea that live beyond the reach of sunlight. But there are still seasons and other cycles in the ocean depths, and its inhabitants respond to those rhythms. And events, such as mass extinctions, in the past have also left their mark on life in the deep sea, so it is not a timeless realm nor a refuge from planetary catastrophes.

In the upper reaches of the deep sea – the twilight zone where there is still some faint downwelling sunlight – animals may perceive changes in day length that mark the passing of the seasons. But there's a bigger difference between seasons than day length, and it reaches deeper than the twilight zone. During springtime at temperate latitudes, there are usually huge blooms of tiny drifting algae at the ocean's surface, which we can see in satellite images as greenish swirls hundreds of kilometres across. As those algae die or get eaten, their remains sink into the deep sea as marine snow, so there's much more food arriving from above during that period every year.

Even at 5,000 metres deep on an abyssal plain, there's a seasonal bonanza of food from the decaying blooms of algae in surface waters. And deep-sea animals make short work of it: timelapse cameras reveal fluffy drifts of marine snow appearing on the seafloor a few weeks after the blooms fade at the surface, and those drifts are then hoovered up in days to weeks by scurrying sea cucumbers and other seabed-dwellers. Some animals then use the energy from that extra food to fuel their reproduction, resulting in seasonal patterns in the lives of some deep-sea species.

Not all areas of the deep sea receive a seasonal deluge of food – there are large equatorial regions where there are no springtime blooms of algae at the ocean's surface. And some deep-sea animals may be indifferent to the arrival of extra food as marine snow once per year because they already have plenty of food all year round. At hydrothermal vents and cold seeps, for example, food is always abundant thanks to the process of chemosynthesis, which enables bacteria to grow using mineral-rich water springing out of the seafloor and thereby provides food for lush colonies of animals. But even in those chemosynthetic habitats, there are still a few animals that reproduce season-ally, such as the shrimp *Alvinocaris stactophila* that lives at cold seeps in the Gulf of Mexico. Females of that species produce their eggs in the autumn and brood them until early spring when they all hatch into larvae. Those larvae feed on marine snow as they drift on ocean currents, and hatching in early spring means there's more food for them to eat as they set out on that journey.

It's not just fluctuations in marine snow that signal the passing of seasons in the deep sea. Winter storms that stir the seas in some regions can be felt in the depths, particularly in submarine canyons on the continental slopes where the storm's push stronger currents along them at that time of year. And there are seasonal cycles in the lives of some deep-sea animals beyond their reproduction. Timelapse cameras left at 1,400 metres deep on the continental slope near Angola over seven years have found that there are more fish cruising over the seabed at that location in November each year. It's likely that some deep-sea fish species follow an annual migration that loops across the ocean floor, similar to the migration of animals, such as wildebeest across the Serengeti plains, but following the seasonal peak in marine snow rather than the rains that nourish those grasslands.

On a much shorter timescale than seasons, tides provide another regular time-signal in the deep sea, with twice-daily, daily, and fortnightly rhythms. The celestial forces that produce tides in the ocean involve more than just the Moon's gravity pulling the water, and the same forces reach into the deep sea as well as moving water on and off our shores. The effect of those forces varies in different regions – in the enclosed Mediterranean Sea, for example, there is very little tide. But in many places in the deep sea the strength and direction of currents flowing over the seafloor varies with the tide, and some animals respond to those regular changes. Swarms of the shrimp *Rimicaris exoculata* shift around the mineral spires of hydrothermal vents on the Mid-Atlantic Ridge as the currents change with the tide, so that they stay on the 'downwind' side of the vents to bathe in the mineral-rich water that they need for their bacteria.

The flow of mineral-rich water out of hydrothermal vents also waxes and wanes over a tidal cycle because of changes in pressure at the seafloor as the sea level above varies with the tide. In thickets of tubeworms at hydrothermal vents in the northeast Pacific, scale-worms and sea spiders crawl up and down the worm tubes as the flow of vent water through the thicket becomes stronger and weaker with the tide. Thanks to the metronome of tides in the ocean, some deep-sea animals may be able to mark the passage of time and possibly coordinate their behaviour. There are hints of a fortnightly tidal pattern in the reproductive cycle of 'palm worms' – a species that looks like a small palm tree – at those same hydrothermal vents 2,200 metres deep in the northeast Pacific. And the rhythm of tides even permeates the cells of some species: by collecting specimens at different times during a day, biologists have found that mussels at hydrothermal vents switch different genes on and off over a tidal cycle, so the tide produces a regular time-signal at a molecular level in those animals.

The cycle of seasons and rhythm of tides show how the deep sea is connected and in sync with the world above. As a result of such connections, the deep sea doesn't offer a refuge from catastrophes, such as the asteroid impact that saw off the dinosaurs sixty-five million years ago – those events make a mark on deep-sea life as well. If a large asteroid slams into the Earth and kicks up dust into the atmosphere that blots out the sun, it not only curbs the growth of plants on land but also algae growing in the surface layer of the ocean, thereby reducing the supply of food sinking into the deep sea. So the deep sea has been affected by mass extinction events that changed life on land – and there have also been some extinction events that have only affected life in the deep.

Several times in the past – and the last time was about fifty-five million years ago – the flow of oxygen-rich water into the deep sea from surface waters in polar regions has waned, sometimes because the continents were in a different configuration that got in the way or because the climate was warmer, both of which can alter ocean circulation. During these times when the deep sea was starved of oxygen, the animals down there may have died out, as all of them – even those thriving in chemosynthetic environments – need oxygen to survive. There's some debate about whether these 'ocean anoxic' events were planet-wide or only affected some regions, but the deep sea has suffered its own extinction events as a result of them, separate from the mass extinctions that also affected life on land.

Life continued in the shallows during ocean anoxic events, and then recolonised the depths once deep-sea circulation started up again and restored the flow of oxygen. One quirk of that history is that some deep-sea animals are very different in size to their shallow-water relatives. Most deep-sea species are smaller than their shallow-water relatives, because there tends to be less food available in the deep sea. But a few are giants in comparison: for example, the deep sea is home to giant squid that can reach 15 metres long, giant sea spiders that have 40-centimetre leg-spans, and giant isopod crustaceans that are ten times the size of shallow species. When ancestral species recolonised the empty deep sea after an ocean anoxic event, they were not hemmed in by competitors, which allowed some of them to evolve into species radically different in size to the species that continued to evolve in crowded shallow waters.

Today the flow of oxygen-rich water into the deep sea is weakening because of changes that we have wrought by the climate. The past can give us clues to the future, and the history of ocean anoxic events should caution us that life in the deep sea is connected to the rest of our world and is particularly sensitive to changes in ocean circulation.

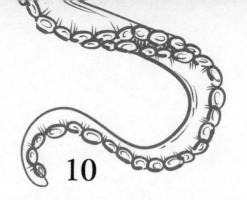

10

Nowhere Is Out of Reach for Us to Explore – nor Untouched by the Impacts of Our Lives

I'm sitting on a bus in the UK city of Southampton looking at my smartphone, which is showing a live video from a Remotely Operated Vehicle (ROV) far beneath a research ship in the middle of the Atlantic. The ROV is exploring a cluster of hydrothermal vents that an expedition has just discovered nearly 2,000 metres deep on the seafloor. The images from the vehicle's cameras are being relayed instantly up its tether cable to the ship, transmitted from ship to shore via a satellite, and streamed live on the internet to anyone with a web browser. Controlled by the team on the ship, the ROV slowly drops down one of the spires of the hydrothermal vents, from the black smoke gushing out of its peak, past swarms of pale shrimp, to blocks of orange-coloured minerals where eel-like fish seem to be basking.

I glance at my phone's clock which shows that it's 2pm UK time, so I tap in another web address to watch live images from a camera on the ocean floor in the Pacific, which is connected to shore by hundreds of kilometres of fibre-optic cable laid across the seabed. Every four hours, this seafloor observatory switches on its lights and camera for four minutes, so that anyone online can watch a close-up view of the animals at another cluster of hydrothermal vents there, at just over 2,000 metres deep. Tubeworms poke their red plumes out of pipe-like yellowish tubes, while purple scaleworms with rows of overlapping armour plates along their backs crawl among them. Next to them are long white hairs made of bacteria, which waft in the shimmering warm water seeping out of the mineral spire that the camera is watching.

As the bus reaches my stop, I tap in another web address, and when I step off and walk along the street my earpods are filled with sounds relayed from an underwater microphone nearly 900 metres deep in Monterey Bay off the coast of California. The buildings and people around me almost fade out as my head is transported into the deep sea an ocean away. I can hear that it's raining there, from a soft hiss of raindrops at the surface. There's a distant low thrum – probably the propellers of a freighter making an early morning run nearby. And then there are the trumpet-like groaning calls of humpback whales, who arrived a month ago with their calves to feast on shoaling fish in undersea canyons.

At the same moment that I'm walking along the street, the sleek 1.3 metre-high yellow tube of an Argo float rises slowly to the surface of the Indian Ocean through the slanting rays of the setting sun, having just completed a dip to 2,000 metres deep. Once its antenna bobs clear of the water, it squirts the payload of measurements recorded by its sensors to a satellite, which beams them to a data store ashore. Within a day or so, after a team of researchers has wrangled the data into a manageable format, those measurements of temperature, salinity, and water density in the deep ocean will also be available to browse on a website. And it's just one of nearly 4,000 such floats drifting through the deep sea around the world right now, monitoring its changing conditions.

The deep sea may seem distant to us, but we have never been so connected to it as we are now. The websites I've described are just a few of many that are freely available to anyone with internet access – the depths of the ocean are literally at our fingertips. And nowhere in the deep sea is out-of-reach for our undersea vehicles. There are two Human-Occupied Vehicles (HOVs) currently in service that can take people to the bottom of the deepest ocean trenches. The *Limiting Factor* HOV was built for a billionaire who became the first person to visit the deepest point in all five oceans in 2019, and it has since dived in many of the trenches around the world, sometimes with scientists aboard. The sub has now been renamed the *Bakunawa* after being sold to another billionaire, who is also funding some scientists to continue using it. Meanwhile, China's new *Fendouzhe* ('Striver') HOV, which carries three people, dived eight times to the bottom of the Mariana Trench in 2020.

There are lots of other tools besides Human Occupied Vehicles in today's toolbox for exploring the deep sea. The first Remotely Operated Vehicle (ROV) to reach the deepest point in the ocean was Japan's *Kaiko* ROV, which also became the first vehicle to dive there repeatedly, making nineteen dives to the Challenger Deep of the Mariana Trench between 1995 and 1998. Those dives collected samples including seafloor sediments, microbes, and a 4.5 centimeter-long amphipod crustacean. *Kaiko* also filmed plastic rubbish there at a depth of 10,898 metres on 28 May 1998. And now Autonomous Underwater Vehicles (AUVs), which survey on their own rather than being remote-controlled, have also reached the bottom of the Mariana Trench, with Russia's *Vityaz* AUV diving there in 2020.

Robotic vehicles, such as ROVs and AUVs, are also becoming increasingly sophisticated to help us understand life in the deep. A new vehicle called *Mesobot*, for example, enables biologists to study the behaviours of animals in the mid-water twilight zone of the ocean. *Mesobot*, which was built by engineers at Woods Hole Oceanographic Institution and Monterey Bay Aquarium Research Institute, can be remotely controlled via a cable to find an animal of interest, then released to follow that animal automatically for up to twenty-four hours. The vehicle uses on-board artificial intelligence to recognise and track its target, and it can film animals using red lighting that doesn't disturb most deep-sea life. Similar artificial intelligence tools are also helping biologists to analyse the many hours of video recorded by deep-diving vehicles on expeditions, greatly speeding up the task of identifying the different types of animals seen during dives to figure out who lives where, and why, in the deep sea.

The technology to explore the deep sea has so far been the privilege of the wealthy nations or individuals, but new equipment may help more people explore the deep sea close to them. *Maka Niu* – which means 'coconut eye' in Hawaiian – is a deep-sea camera system with sensors that measure environmental conditions, and it can be deployed from a small boat to reach 1,500 metres deep. The system was designed collaboratively by the non-profit Ocean Discovery League with scientists, teachers, fishers and local community groups on the coasts of eleven countries. The design costs around 700 US dollars to build, which should help to equip a new, wider generation of deep-sea explorers.

But at the same time that the deep sea has become more accessible to us, our lives have already had an impact on it, even in its deepest reaches. The deep sea may seem like another world because its conditions are so different to our world above the waves, but its deepest point is less than 11 kilometres from the surface – the same distance as a comfortable two-hour stroll on land. I live about the same distance from a railway, and on a still night I can hear freight wagons clattering along it – so it's not surprising that an underwater microphone at the bottom of the Mariana Trench has picked up noise from shipping, particularly as sound travels much better through water than through air. And noise pollution is not our only pervasive impact in the deep sea.

Human rubbish has also reached the deepest places in the ocean. Dives into the trenches have found visible items, such as plastic bags, along with telltale marks that items can leave as they drift across the soft-sedimented seafloor. In addition to the detritus that we can see, tiny particles of microplastics also sink to the ocean floor along with marine snow, turning up in sediment samples from the bottom of the deep trenches. And in 2020, a team of scientists found a microplastic fibre in the gut of a previously unknown species of amphipod crustacean living at nearly 7,000 metres deep in the Mariana Trench, which they named *Eurythenes plasticus* to highlight the problem of plastic pollution.

Advances in technology have also enabled us to extract resources, such as fossil fuels, and fish from greater depths. In 2016, the drillship *Maersk Venturer* drilled an oil well-head on the seafloor at a depth of 3,400 metres off the coast of Uraguay, setting a new record for deep-sea oil and gas operations. During the late twentieth century, fisheries also expanded into the deep sea, targeting species, such as the orange roughy *Hoplostethus atlanticus*. But some deep-sea fish species, such as the orange roughy, take decades to grow and reproduce, which can make them particularly vulnerable to overfishing. And techniques, such as bottom-trawling, which scrapes life off the seafloor with weighted nets, can also destroy deep-sea coral and sponge beds that take thousands of years to grow and provide shelter for lots of other types of animals. But effective fisheries management has halted the decline of some deep-sea fish stocks, and in 2022 the European Union banned deep-sea bottom-trawling at eighty-seven sites spanning 16,000 square kilometres in the northeast Atlantic, showing how regulation can help to protect the deep sea.

Meanwhile, a new industry is poised to begin in the deep sea, with the development of seafloor mining for deposits of metals, such as cobalt, that are needed in low-carbon technology, such as electric vehicle batteries. In 1994, the United Nations created an organisation called the International Seabed Authority to figure out how to share potential benefits from deep-sea mining with people around the world, because most of the mineral deposits on the ocean floor lie beyond the boundaries of any nation's jurisdiction. But several nations involved in discussions at the UN body are now calling for a halt in the development of this new industry, so that scientists can find out more about its likely environmental impacts to help decide how it should be regulated before mining begins.

Out of all our impacts on the deep sea, however, climate change is the most pervasive and perhaps the most difficult to tackle. The greenhouse gases that we add to the atmosphere initially trap more heat there, but that extra heat doesn't stay in the atmosphere. More than 90 per cent of it gets transferred to the ocean, with several knock-on effects that reach the deep sea and its inhabitants, from altering the chemistry of seawater to changing the amount of food that sinks to the ocean floor.

In particular, the amount of oxygen in the deep sea – on which all its animals depend – is declining because of a triple-whammy of effects from ocean warming. Firstly, warmer waters contain less oxygen because the amount that can dissolve in it decreases as temperature increases. Secondly, exacerbating that effect, the metabolisms of deep-sea organisms also run faster at higher temperatures, using up oxygen more quickly. And finally, the ocean currents that sink from polar regions to spill out across the deep ocean, carrying oxygen from the atmosphere into the deep, are getting weaker as polar ice melts. The deep sea is already on course to end up with 10 per cent less oxygen overall than it had in pre-industrial times, and every day that we delay in achieving 'net zero' in greenhouse gas emissions simply worsens that impact even further.

With the technology that we now have and the growing awareness of our impacts, it's important to ask why we explore the deep sea – for whose benefit? Are we exploring to understand more about its role in our planet's life-support system, and help people to make more informed choices that benefit all of us? Or are we exploring to exploit its resources for the benefit of some people more than others? And who is exploring – is it a few rich people who have the resources to do so with their chosen guests, or are we creating ways for anyone to be a partner in it, harnessing the power of our different perspectives? The challenge of exploring the deep sea is now more social than technological – and how we proceed will test whether our species has what it takes to overcome the wider challenges that we face on this astonishing deep-sea planet.

Acknowledgements

This book owes its existence to its editor, George Brooker – thank you, George, for inviting me to contribute to this series, and for your insights and patience during preparation and publication. And I would like to thank the team at Orion Books for making the details run so smoothly throughout.

I am grateful to the worldwide community of scientists who are pushing back the boundary of what we know about the deep sea every day. I'm very fortunate to work with some of them directly, and am continually amazed at how the field of deep-sea research has grown over the past twenty-five years. I've not named the many scientists whose discoveries are mentioned in each chapter, or referenced their research papers, as it's not that kind of book. I'd like to apologise for that to all those colleagues, without whom this book wouldn't exist. And any errors in summarising the findings of their studies are entirely mine.

I would also like to thank my students for keeping my passion for the deep sea alive. Each year I enjoy updating my deep-sea ecology class to include the latest advances and try to put them into a big picture that makes sense. Teaching that course always expands my perspective, and it's great to watch students develop their own passion for the deep sea and challenge the why, how, with and for whom we explore it. The future of deep-sea exploration belongs to them, and I think it's in good hands.

As always, I owe everything I do to Claire and Zena, through their support and the motivation that they inspire, and for the biggest voyage of exploration that we undertake in our lives together.